Name _____

Time to Eat

Follow each path with a crayon.

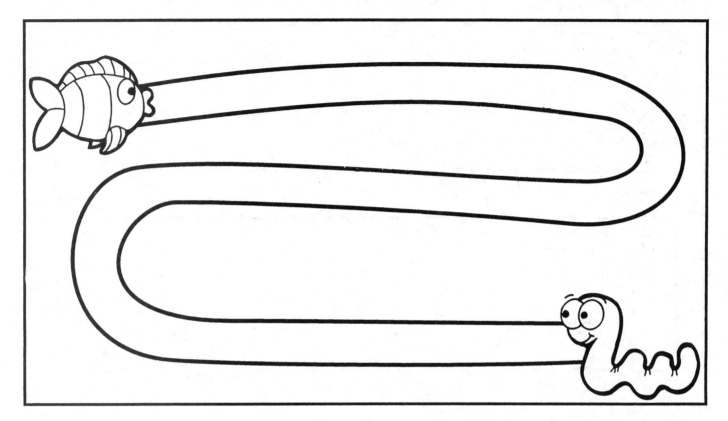

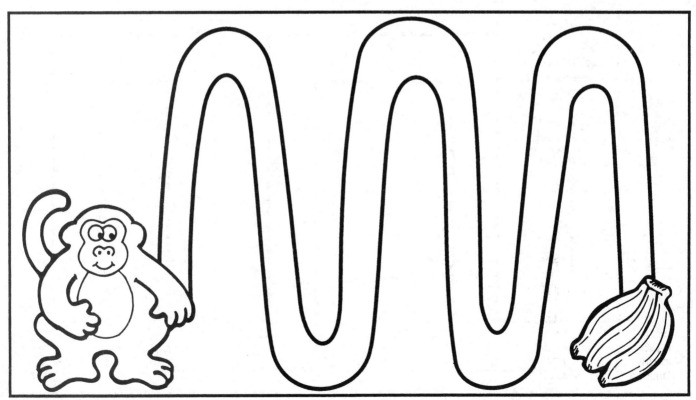

1

FS-32062 Beginning Manuscript Handwriting

Going Home

Follow each path with a crayon.

FS-32062 Beginning Manuscript Handwriting

Matching Shapes

Trace the lines from left to right.

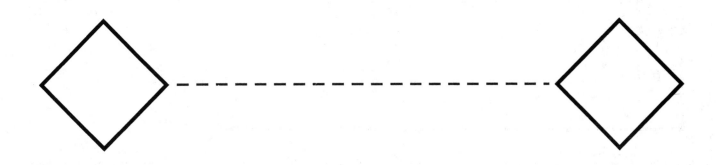

Playing Sports

Trace the lines from left to right.

4

On the Go

Trace the lines from left to right.

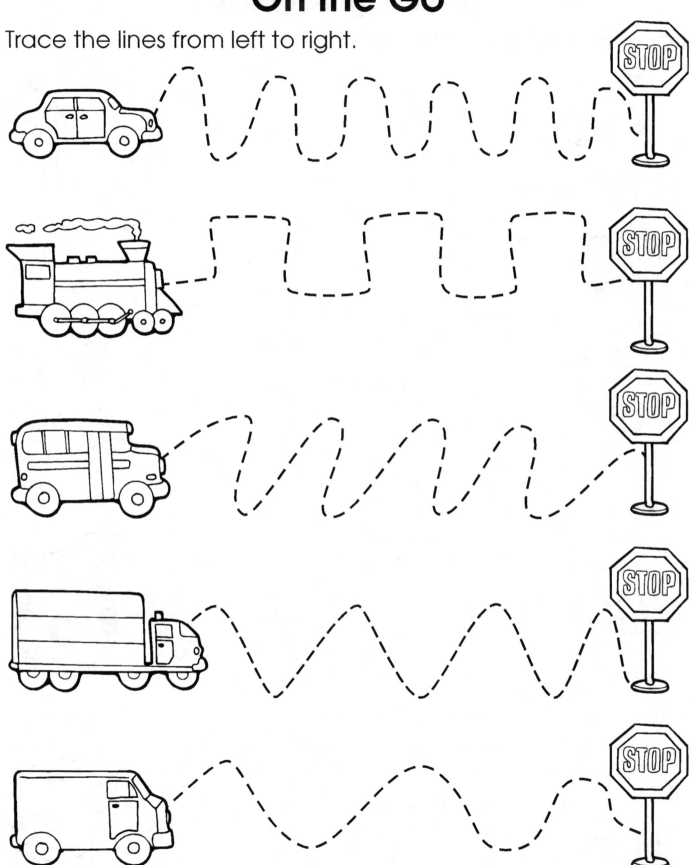

Find the Rhyme

Trace the lines from left to right.

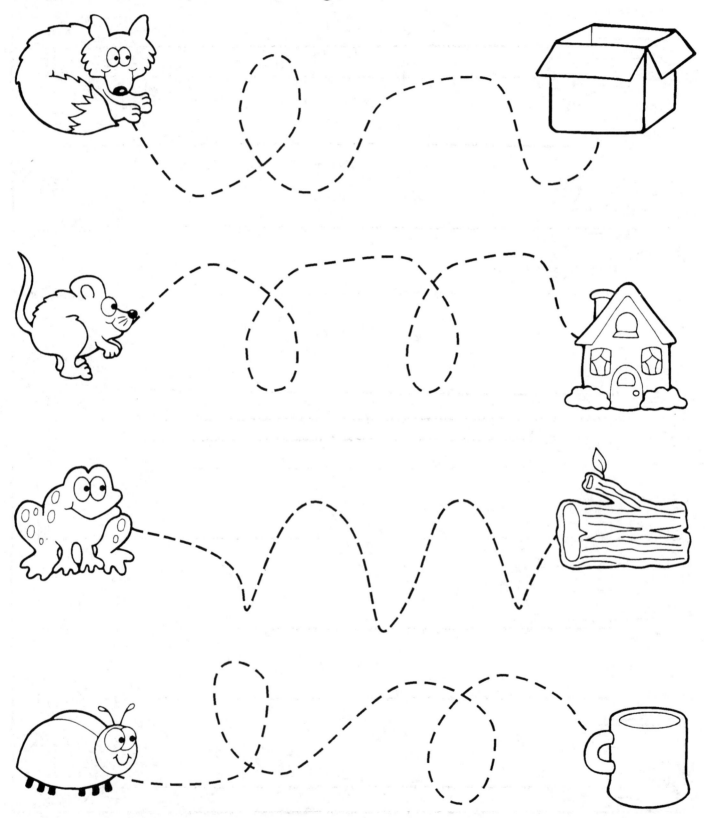

Moving Along

Trace each line carefully. Do not lift your pencil until you get to the stop sign.

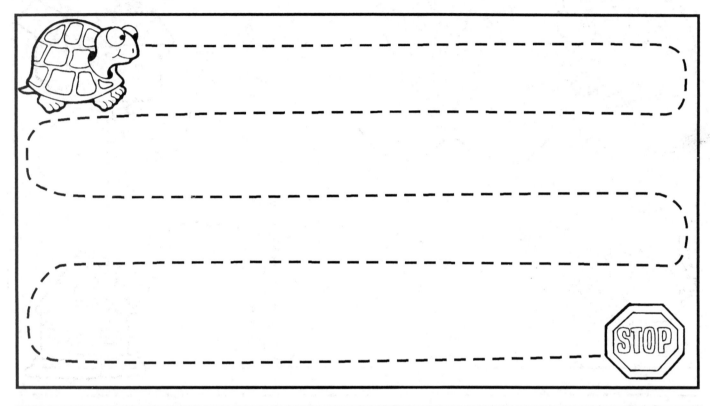

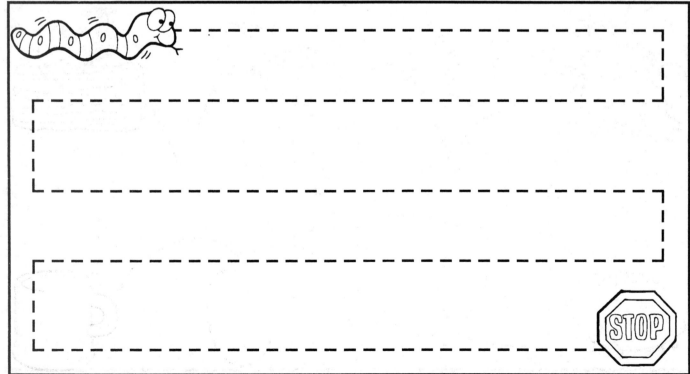

FS-32062 Beginning Manuscript Handwriting

Name_____

Flying South

Trace the lines from top to bottom.

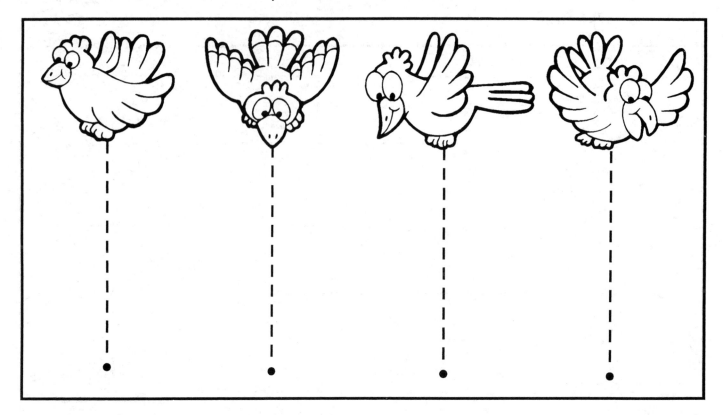

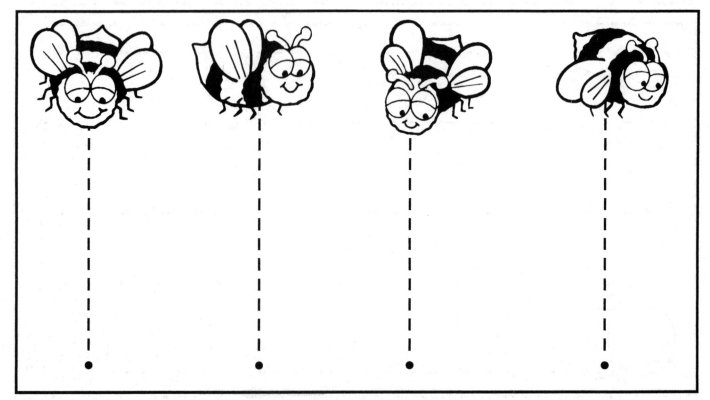

FS-32062 Beginning Manuscript Handwriting

More Than One

Trace the lines from top to bottom.

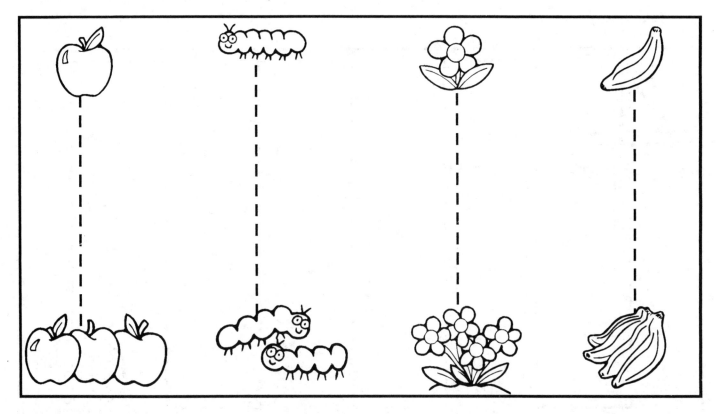

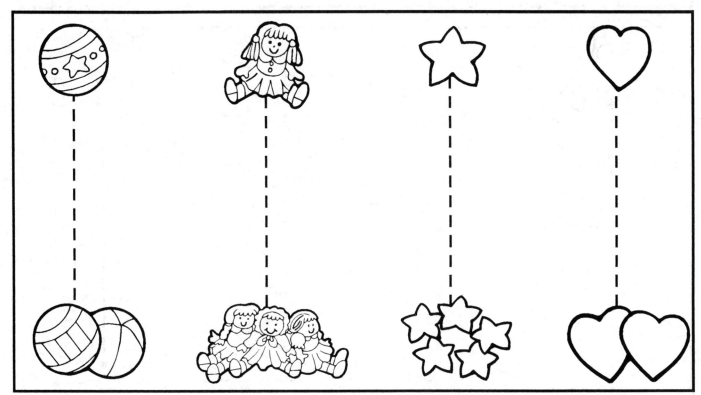

FS-32062 Beginning Manuscript Handwriting

Follow the Path

Trace each line carefully. Do not lift your pencil until you get to the stop sign.

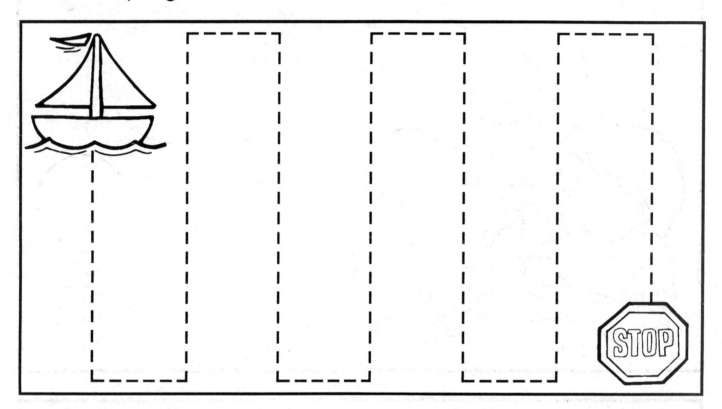

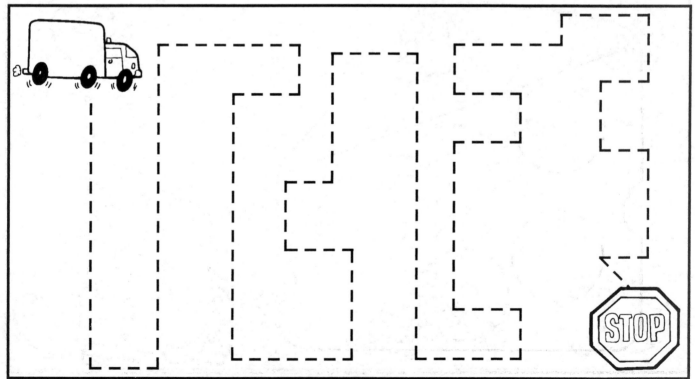

10

Name _____

Circles

Trace the circles. Color the pictures.

11

FS-32062 Beginning Manuscript Handwriting

Name _____

Squares

Trace the squares. Color the pictures.

12

FS-32062 Beginning Manuscript Handwriting

Triangles

Trace the triangles. Color the pictures.

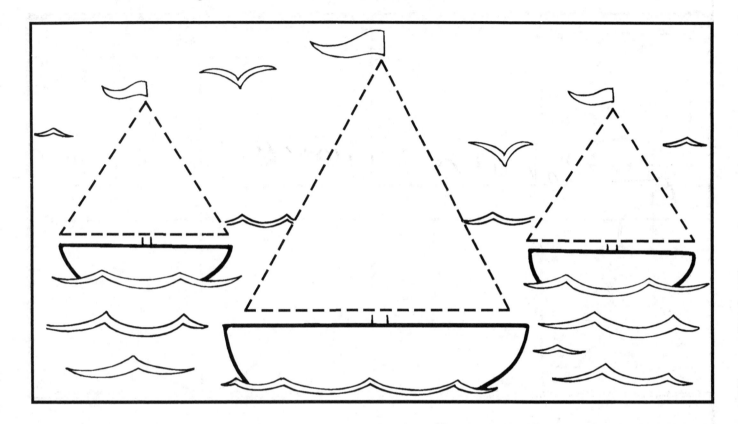

Drawing Shapes

Trace the shapes. Draw each shape three times.

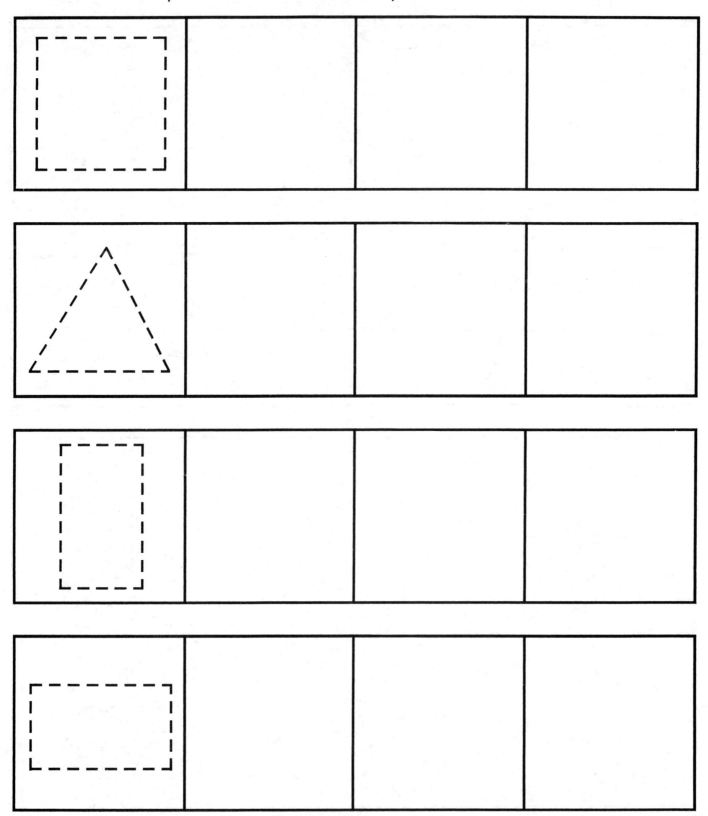

14

FS-32062 Beginning Manuscript Handwriting

More Shapes

Trace the shapes. Draw each shape three times.

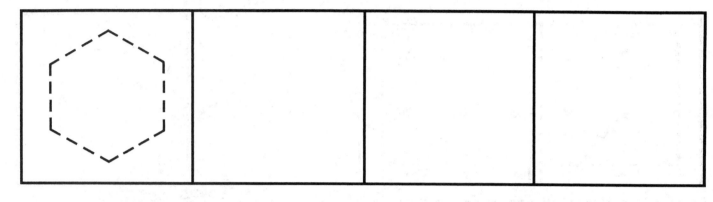

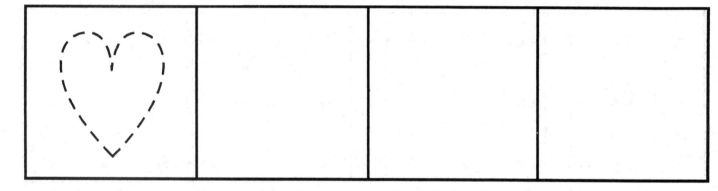

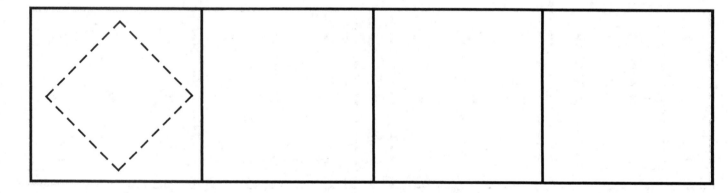

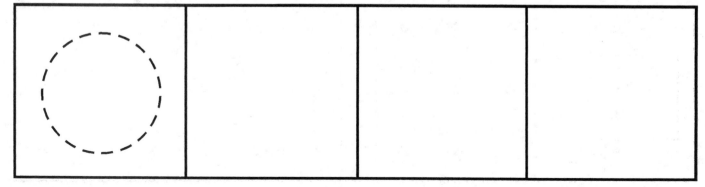

15

Name_____

Connect the Dots

Copy the patterns shown.

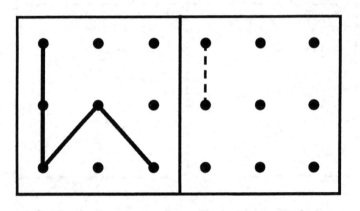

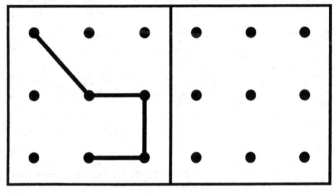

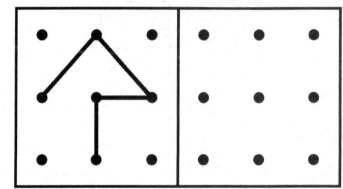

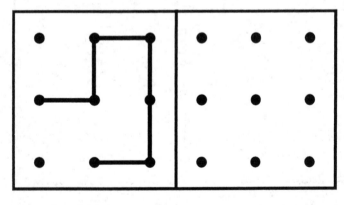

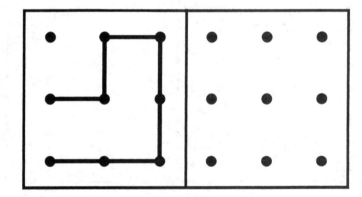

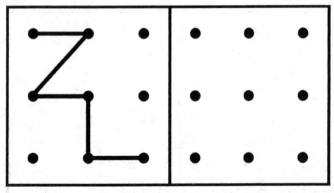

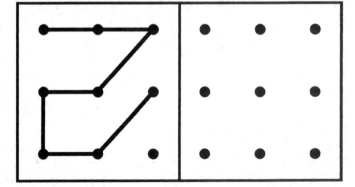

FS-32062 Beginning Manuscript Handwriting

Find a Match

In each box, draw lines to match the pictures.

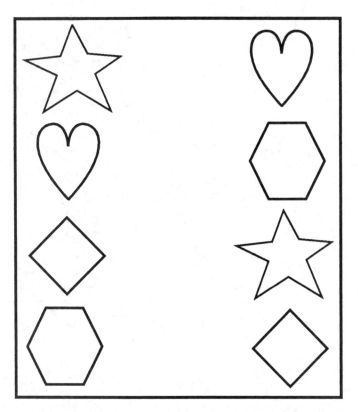

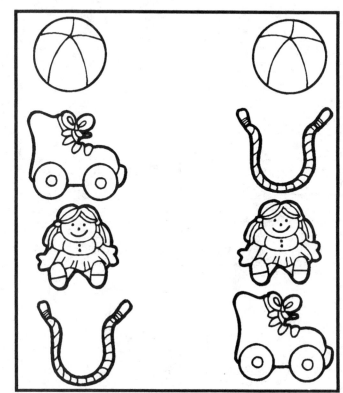

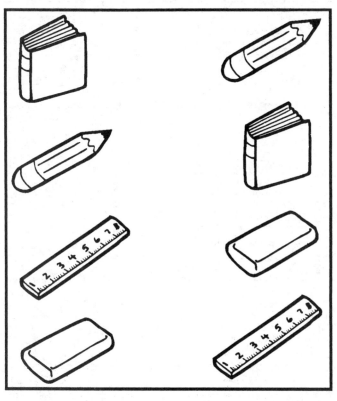

FS-32062 Beginning Manuscript Handwriting

Tracing Aa and Bb

Tracing Cc and Dd

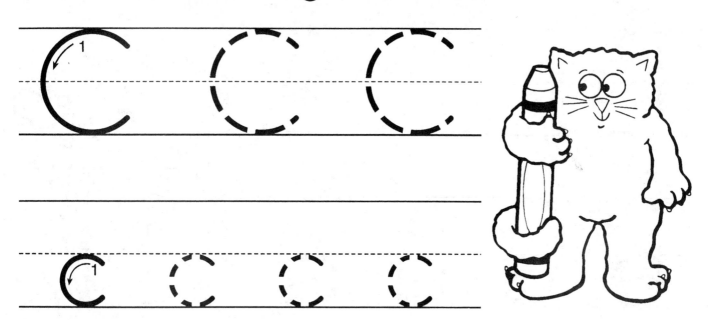

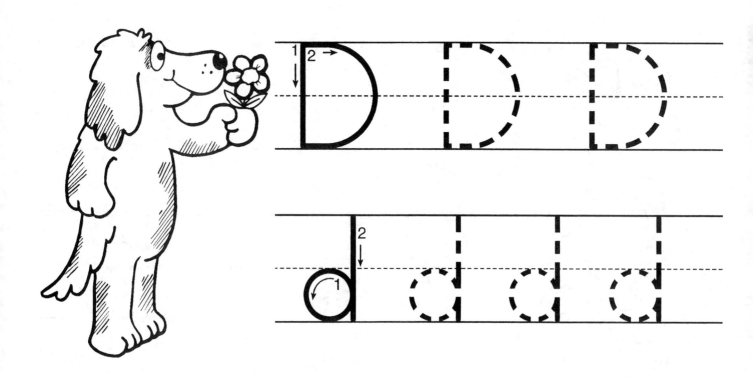

Name_____

Tracing Ee and Ff

FS-32062 Beginning Manuscript Handwriting

Name_____

Tracing Gg and Hh

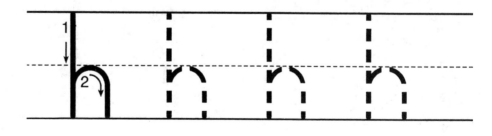

21

Tracing Ii and Jj

FS-32062 Beginning Manuscript Handwriting

Tracing Kk and Ll

FS-32062 Beginning Manuscript Handwriting

Name

Tracing Mm and Nn

FS-32062 Beginning Manuscript Handwriting

Tracing Oo and Pp

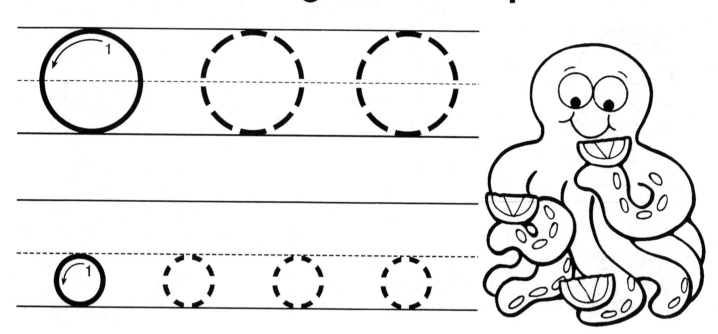

25

Name

Tracing Qq and Rr

FS-32062 Beginning Manuscript Handwriting

Tracing Ss and Tt

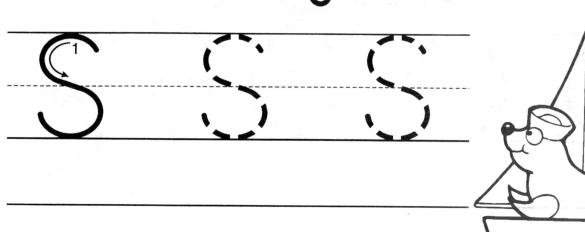

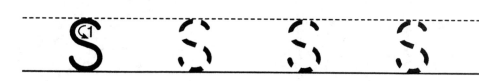

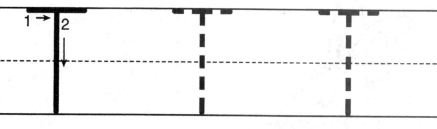

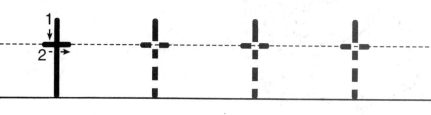

FS-32062 Beginning Manuscript Handwriting

Tracing Uu and Vv

FS-32062 Beginning Manuscript Handwriting

Tracing Ww and Xx

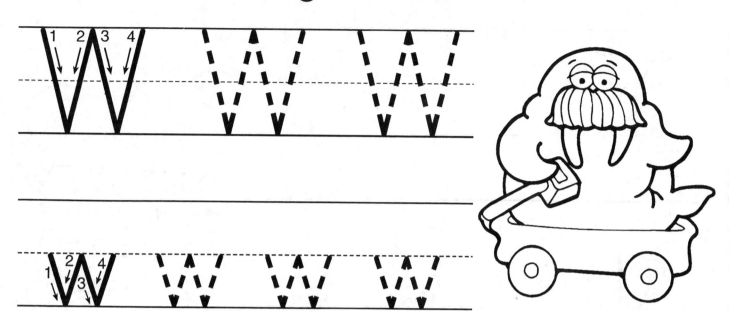

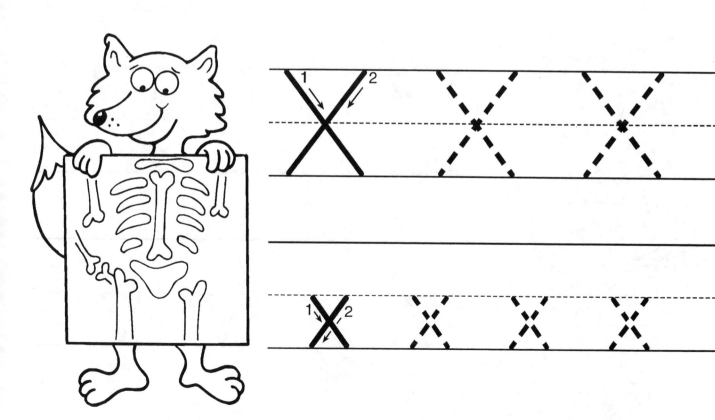

FS-32062 Beginning Manuscript Handwriting

Tracing Yy and Zz

Tracing A to Z

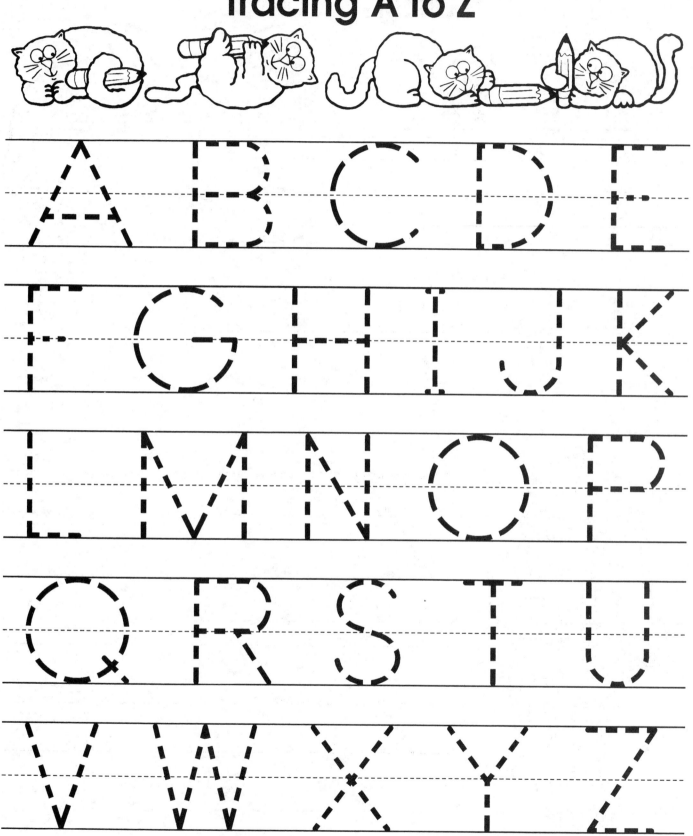

A B C D E

F G H I J K

L M N O P

Q R S T U

V W X Y Z

31

Tracing a to z

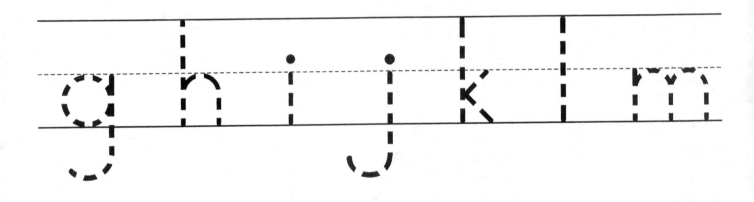

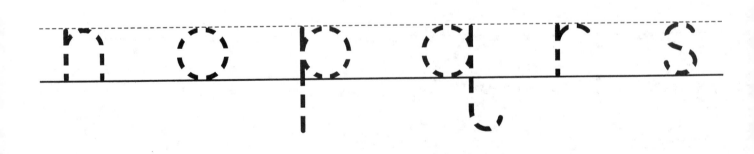

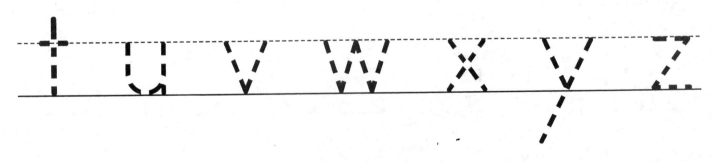

FS-32062 Beginning Manuscript Handwriting

Aa

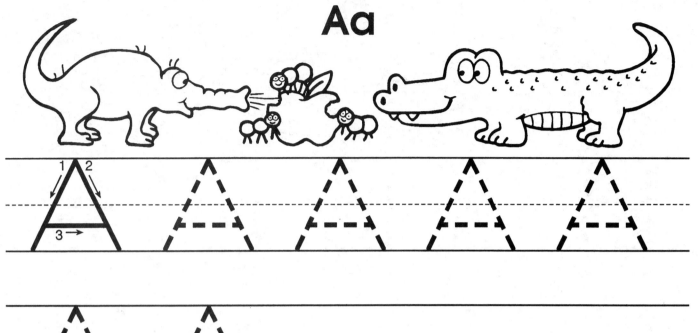

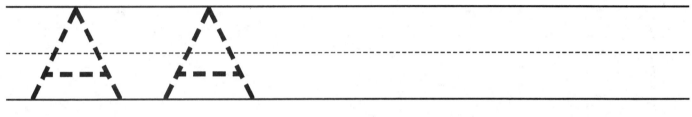

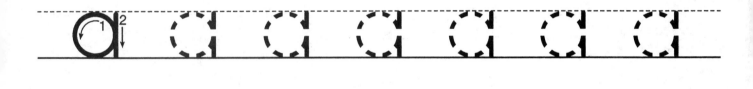

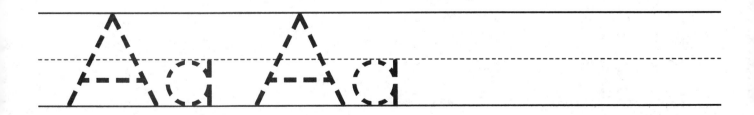

FS-32062 Beginning Manuscript Handwriting

Bb

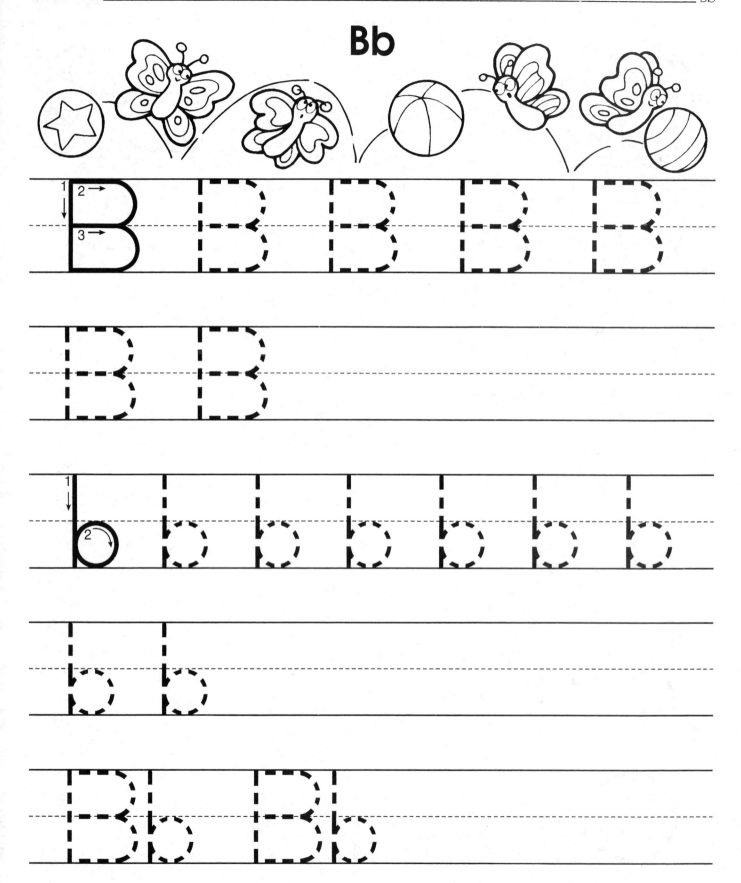

FS-32062 Beginning Manuscript Handwriting

Cc

C C C C C

C C

C C C C C C C

C C

35

FS-32062 Beginning Manuscript Handwriting

Name_____

Dd

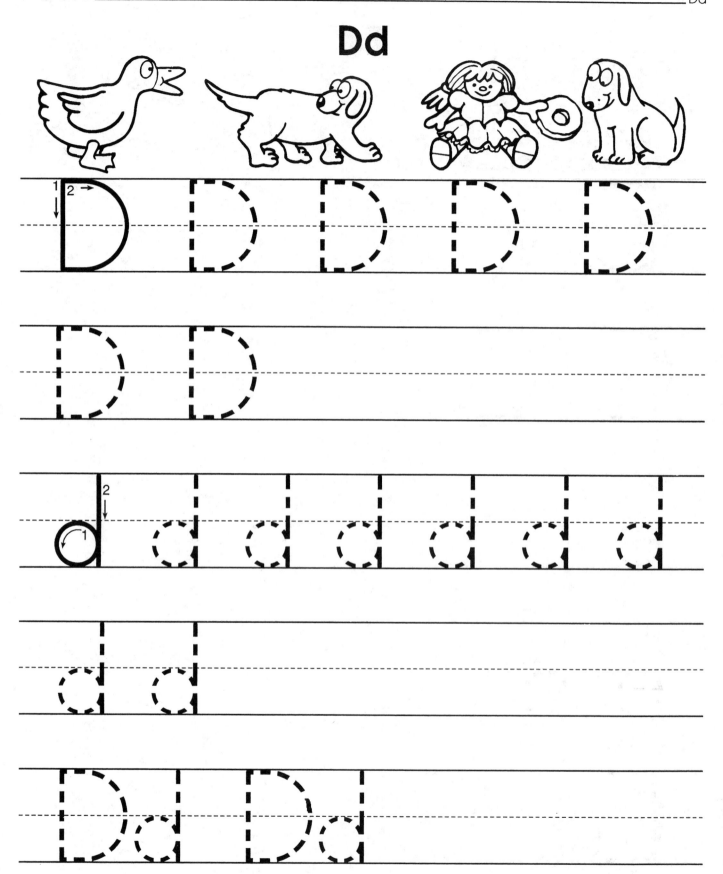

FS-32062 Beginning Manuscript Handwriting

Ee

37

Ff

38

Gg

G G G G G G

G G

g g g g g g g

g g
Gg Gg

 FS-32062 Beginning Manuscript Handwriting

Hh

40

Ii

FS-32062 Beginning Manuscript Handwriting

Jj

J J J J J

J J

j j j j j j j

j j

j j j j

Name _____

Kk

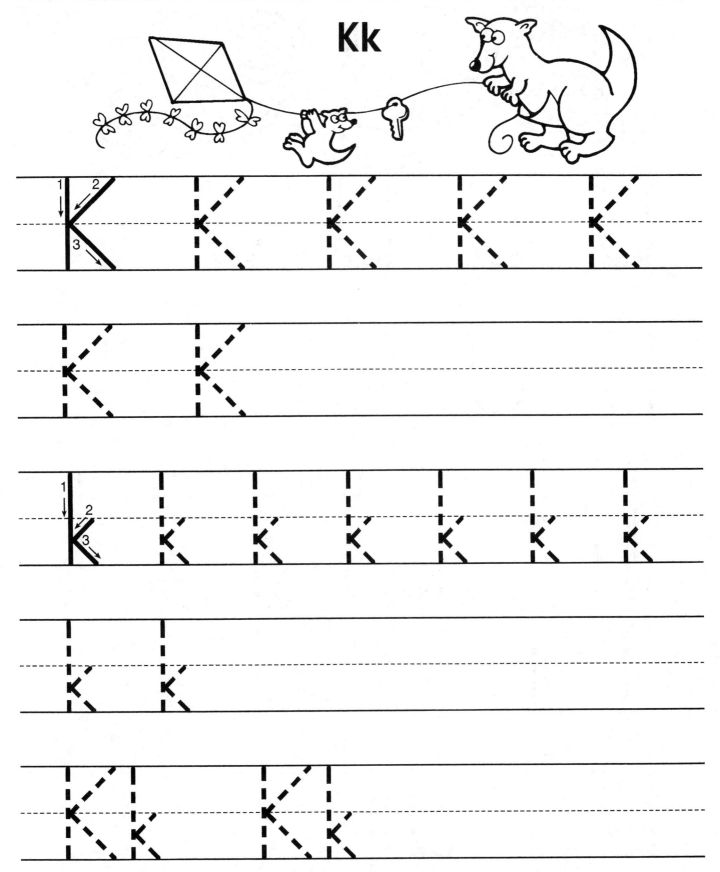

© Frank Schaffer Publications, Inc.   FS-32062 Beginning Manuscript Handwriting

Name

Ll

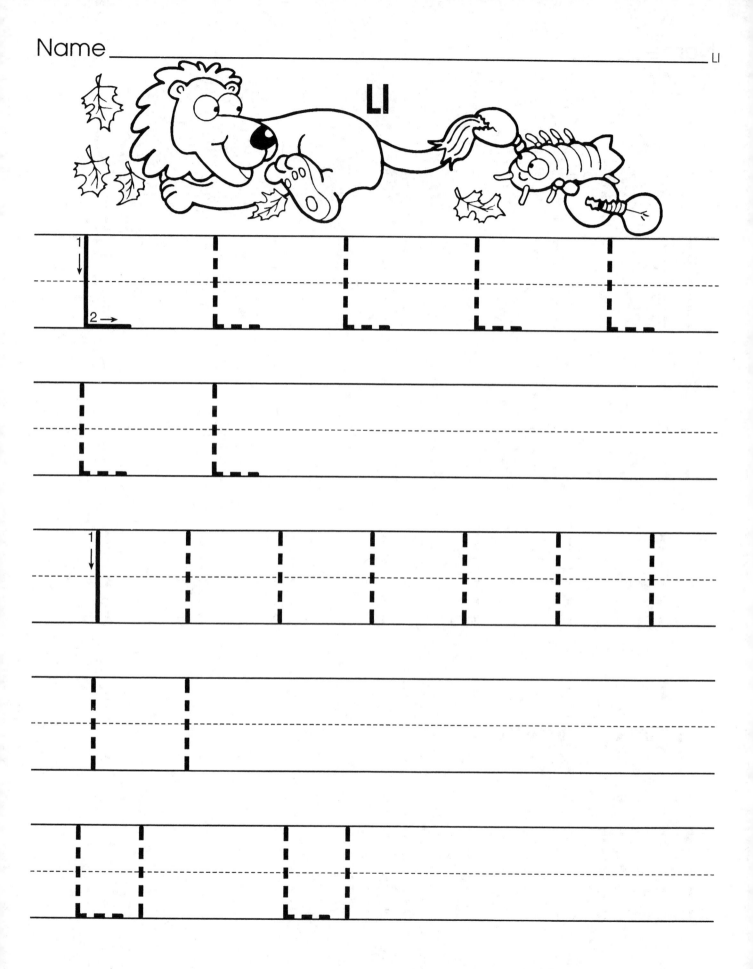

FS-32062 Beginning Manuscript Handwriting

Mm

M M M M M M M

M M

m m m m m m m

m m

Mm Mm

Nn

N N N N N N

N N N

n n n n n n n

n n

N n N n

Oo

FS-32062 Beginning Manuscript Handwriting

Name _____

Pp

P P P P P

P P

P P P P P P P

P P

P P

FS-32062 Beginning Manuscript Handwriting

Qq

Q Q Q Q Q

Q Q

q q q q q q q

q q

Q q Q q

Rr

Ss

FS-32062 Beginning Manuscript Handwriting

Tt

Name _____

Uu

FS-32062 Beginning Manuscript Handwriting

Vv

FS-32062 Beginning Manuscript Handwriting

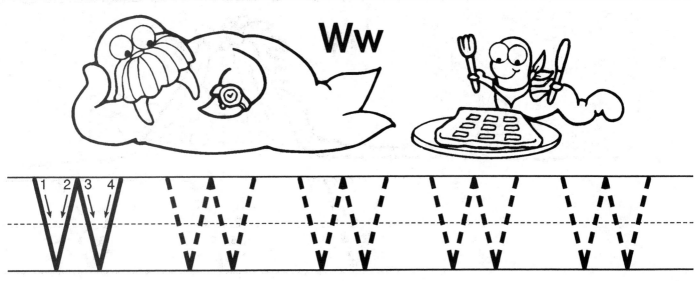

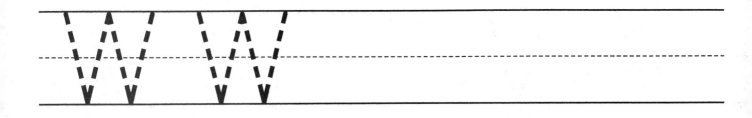

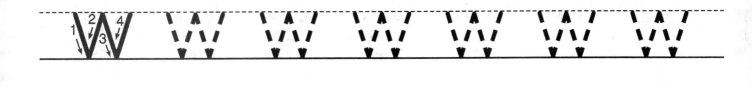

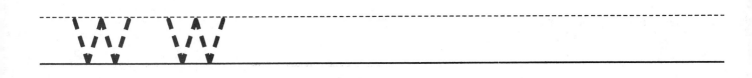

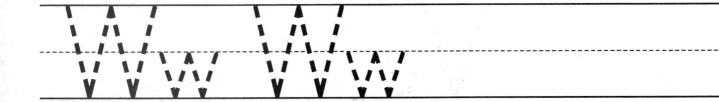

Name _____

© Frank Schaffer Publications, Inc.   FS-32062 Beginning Manuscript Handwriting

Name _____

Yy

Frank Schaffer Publications, Inc.

FS-32062 Beginning Manuscript Handwriting

Name_____

Zz

FS-32062 Beginning Manuscript Handwriting

Name_____

Let's Count

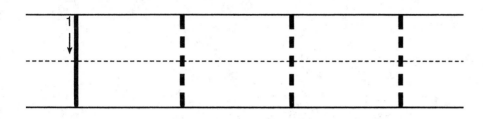 

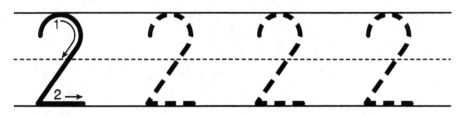 

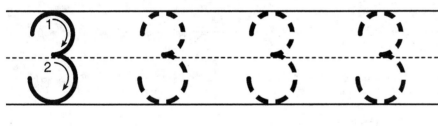 

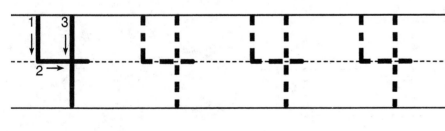 

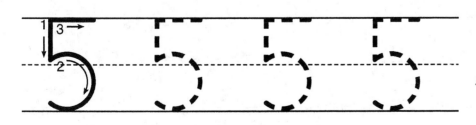 

FS-32062 Beginning Manuscript Handwriting

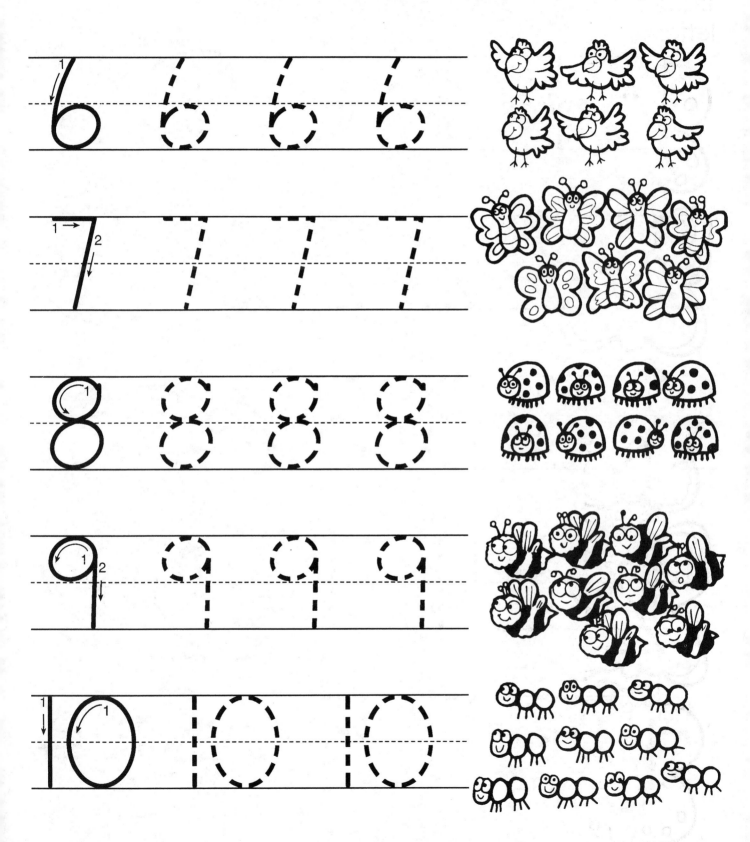

More Counting

Busy Butterflies

Trace the letters. Match the capital letters to the lowercase letters.

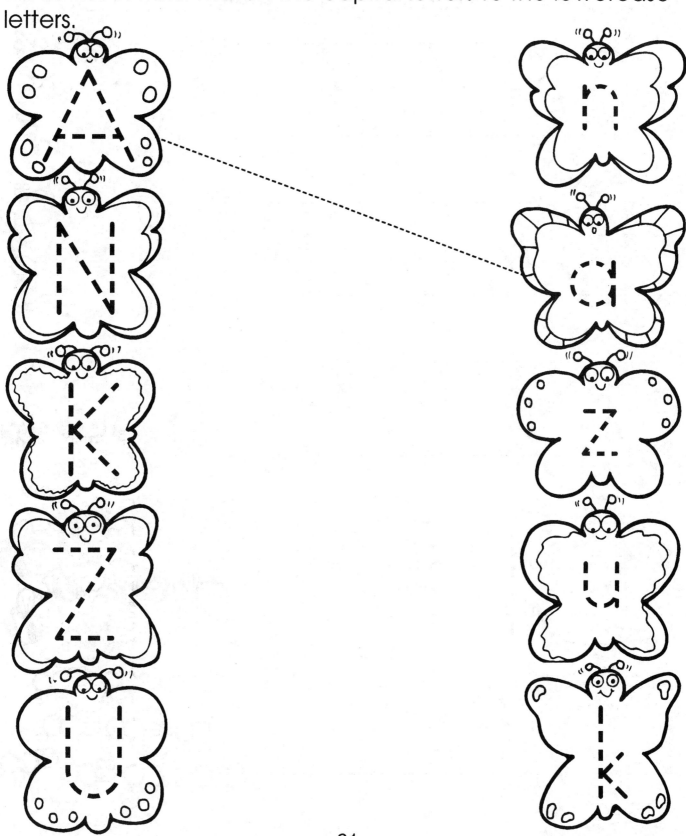

61

FS-32062 Beginning Manuscript Handwriting

Friendly Fish

Trace the letters. Match the capital letters to the lowercase letters.

Hats for You

Write the matching lowercase letters.

Wiggly Worms

Write the matching capital letters.

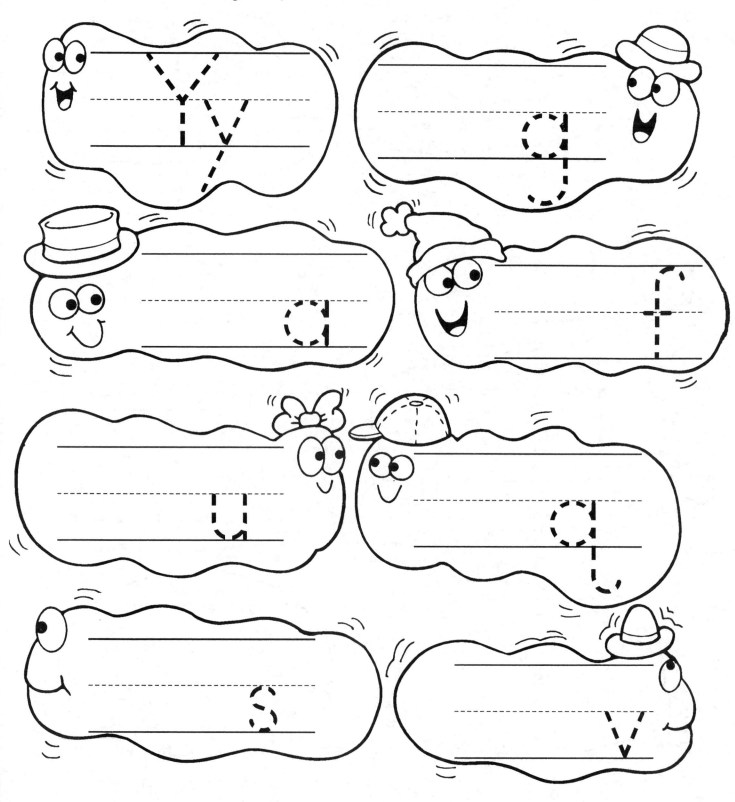

Name _____

Aa

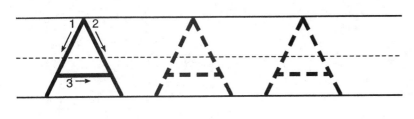

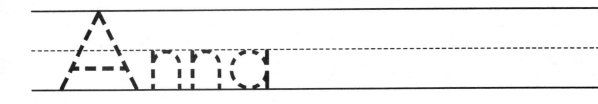

Anna

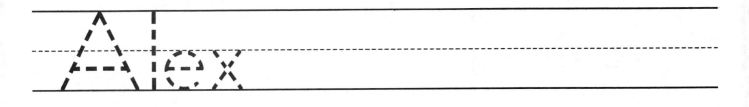

Alex

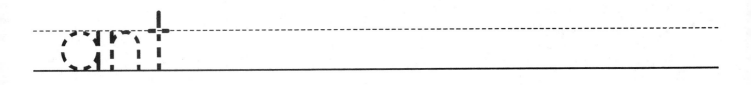

ant

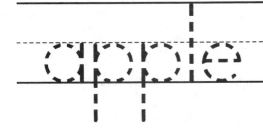

apple

Bb

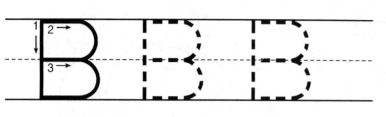

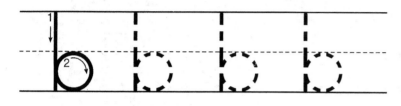

Billy

Belinda

bear

boot

Cc

C C C

c c c c

Carrie

Chris

camel

cake

FS-32062 Beginning Manuscript Handwriting

Name_____ Dd

Dd

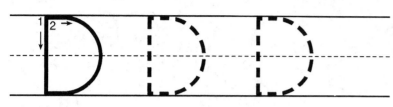

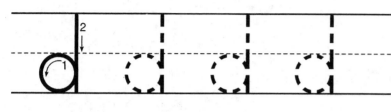

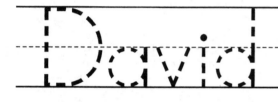

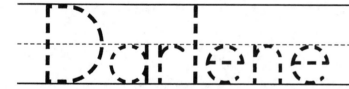

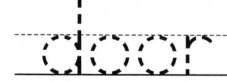

FS-32062 Beginning Manuscript Handwriting

Ee

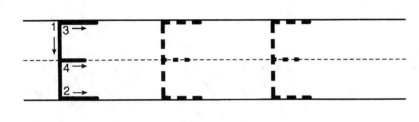

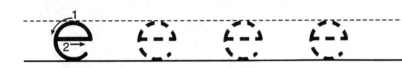

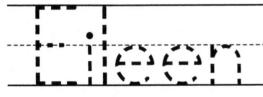

Erik

Eileen

egg

eagle

Ff

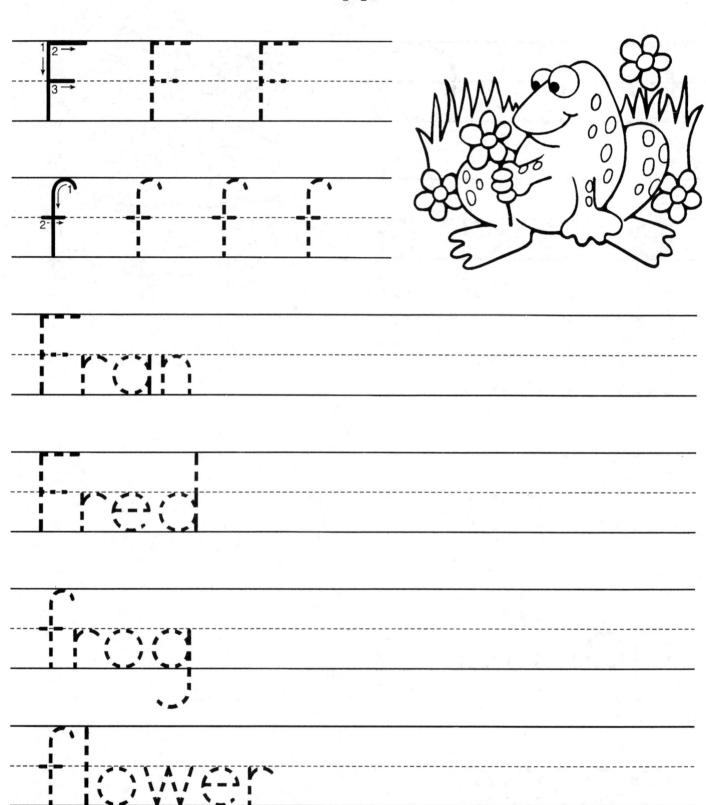

Fran

Fred

frog

flower

Name _____

Gg

G G G G

g g g g

Gina

Greg

gorilla

grape

Hh

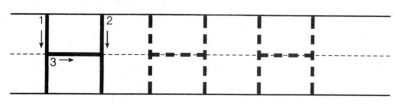

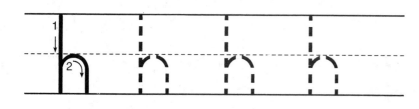

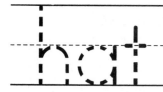

72

FS-32062 Beginning Manuscript Handwriting

Name _____ Ii

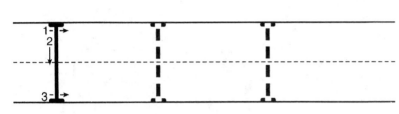

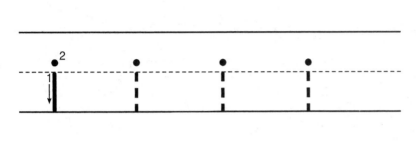

Isaac

Irene

iron

iguana

73

Name _____

Jj

J J J J

j j j j j

Janelle

Jeremy

jet

jaguar

Kk

Keiko

Ken

kite

kitten

75

Ll

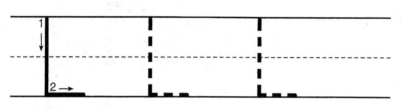

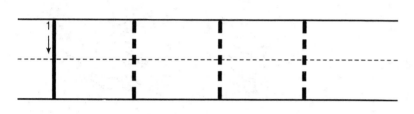

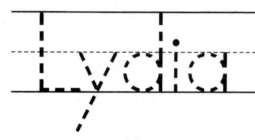

Leo

Lydia

lion

letter

76

Mm

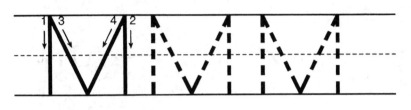

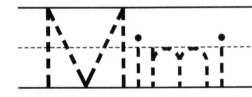

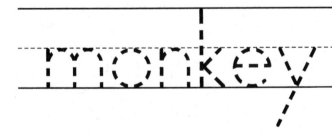

77

FS-32062 Beginning Manuscript Handwriting

Nn

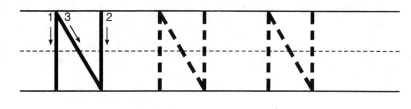

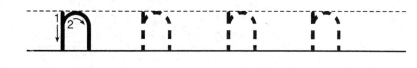

Neil

Nicole

newt

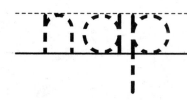

nap

Oo

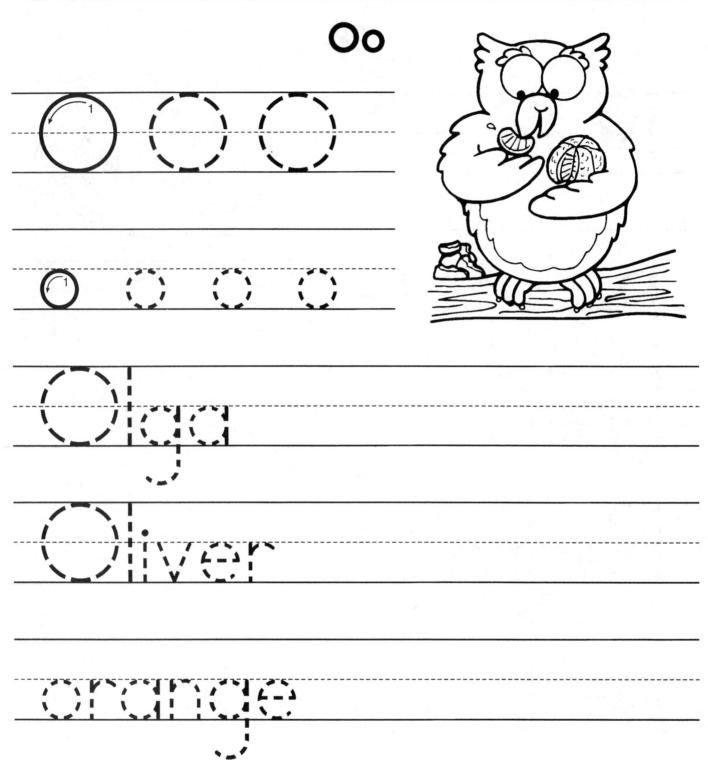

Olga

Oliver

orange

owl

79

FS-32062 Beginning Manuscript Handwriting

Pp

P P P P

P P P P

Polly

Pedro

park

parrot

Qq

Quincy

Quiana

quail

quilt

81

Rr

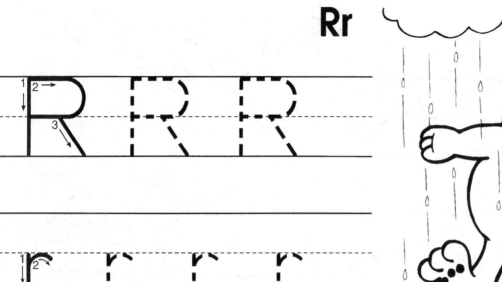

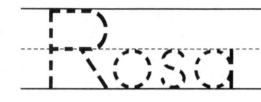

Rosa

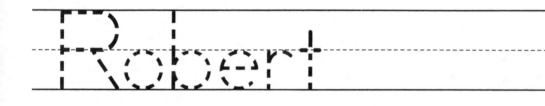

Robert

rain

rabbit

82

Ss

S S S

s s s s

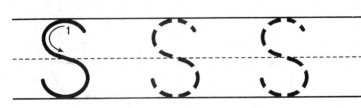

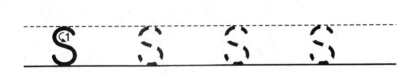

Sergio

Sara

star

snake

Name_____

Tt

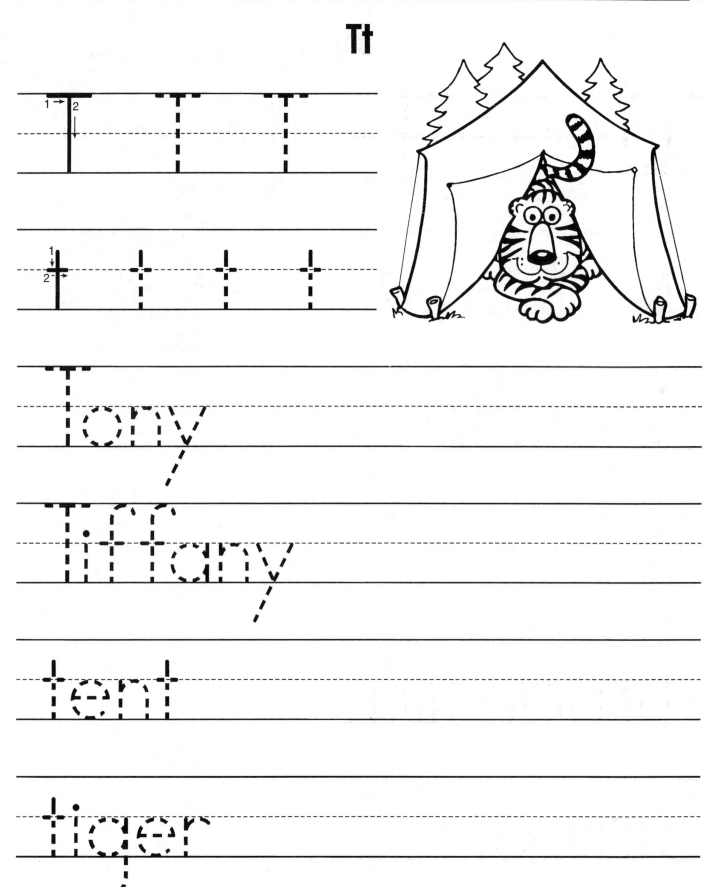

Tony

Tiffany

tent

tiger

Name_____

Uu

U U U

u u u u

Ursula

Ulysses

umbrella

unicorn

Vv

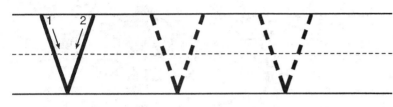

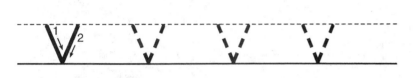

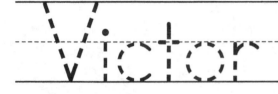

Vera

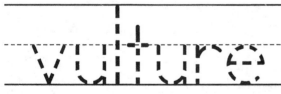

Victor

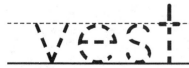

vulture

vest

FS-32062 Beginning Manuscript Handwriting

Ww

W W W W

w w w w

Wayne

Whitney

walrus

watch

Xx

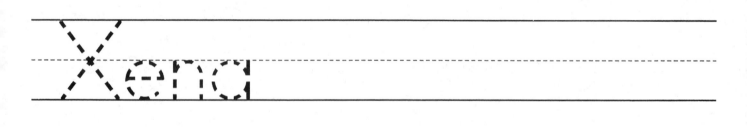

Xavier

Xena

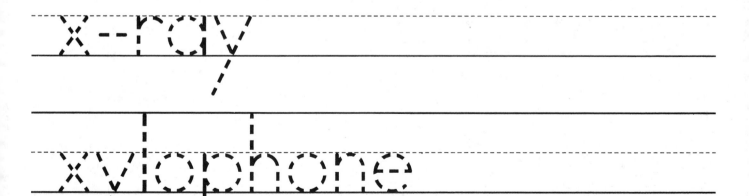

x-ray

xylophone

Yy

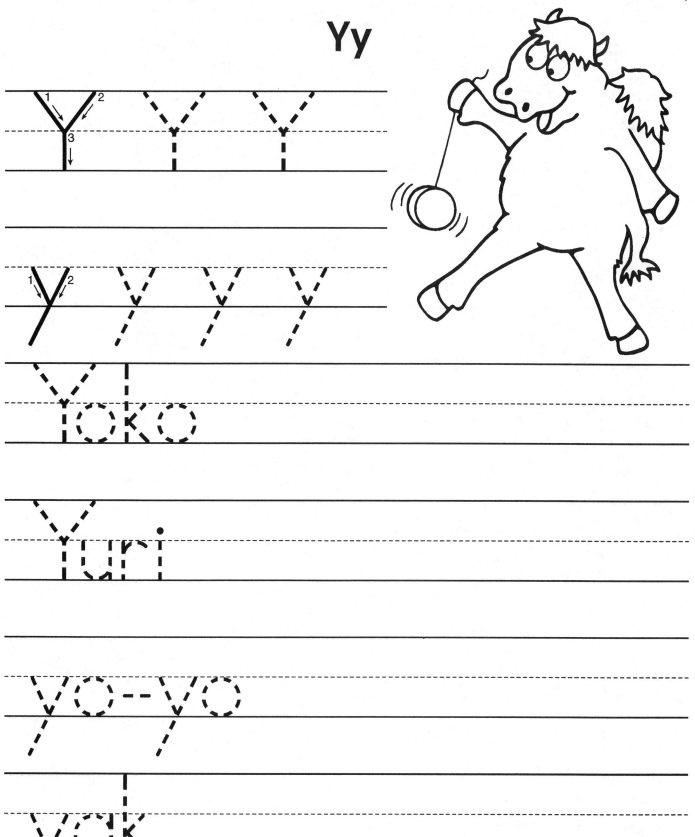

Y Y Y Y

y y y y

Yoko

Yuri

yo-yo

yak

FS-32062 Beginning Manuscript Handwriting

Zz

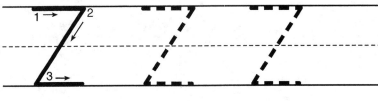

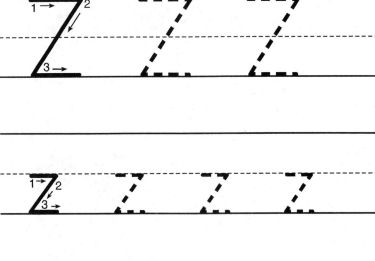

Zoe

Zane

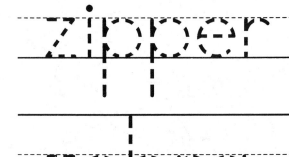

zipper

zebra

Name_____

What's Missing?

Write the capital letters in order.

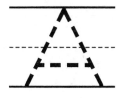   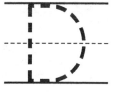 

 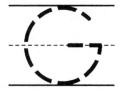  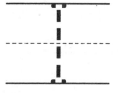 

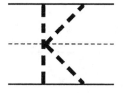 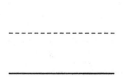  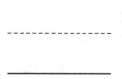 

 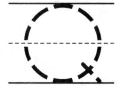 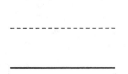 

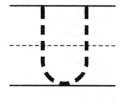 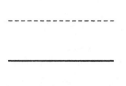 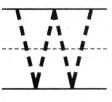

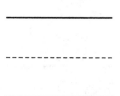 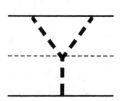  

FS-32062 Beginning Manuscript Handwriting

Writing a to z

Write the lowercase letters in order.

  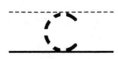  

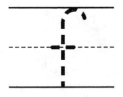  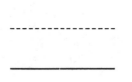 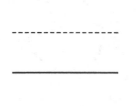 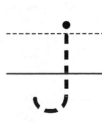

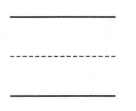 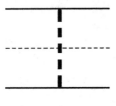 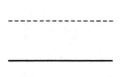  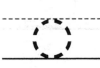

 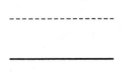 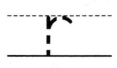  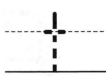

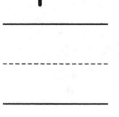 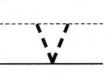 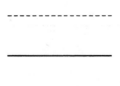 

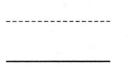

FS-32062 Beginning Manuscript Handwriting

Name_____

Numbers 0–5

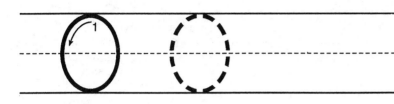

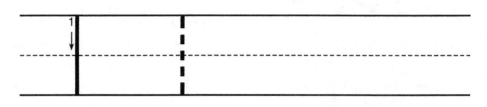

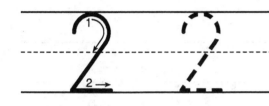

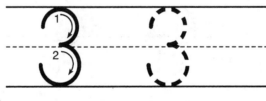

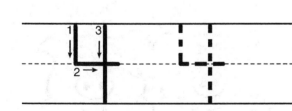

FS-32062 Beginning Manuscript Handwriting

Numbers 6–10

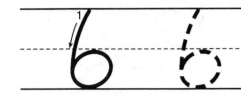 

 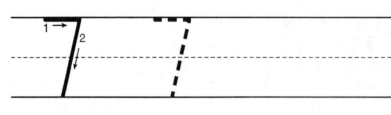

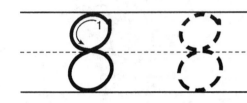 

 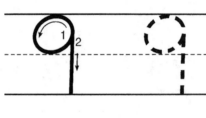

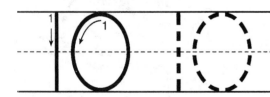 

Write your phone number below.

94

FS-32062 Beginning Manuscript Handwriting

Number Words

zero

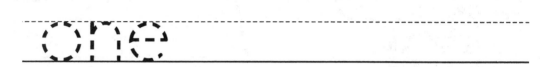
one

two

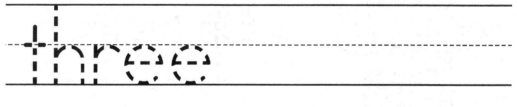
three

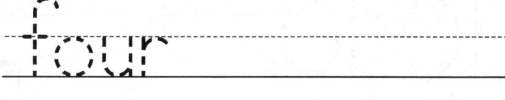
four

five

FS-32062 Beginning Manuscript Handwriting

More Number Words

six

seven

eight

nine

ten

96

FS-32062 Beginning Manuscript Handwriting

Name_____

Aa

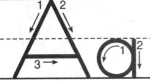

My Best

Aaron

apples

Aaron ate apples.

FS-32062 Beginning Manuscript Handwriting

Name _____

Bb

My Best

bees

buzz

Busy bees buzz.

98   FS-32062 Beginning Manuscript Handwriting

Name_____

Cc

C c

My Best

_____

cats

cakes

Cats cut cakes.

FS-32062 Beginning Manuscript Handwriting

Name _____ Dd

Dd

ducks

dive

Ducks dive deep.

Ee

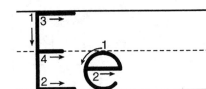

Erin

eggs

Erin eats eggs.

Ff

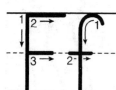

foxes

fish

Five foxes fish.

Gg

My Best

G g

goats

golfing

Goats go golfing.

Hh

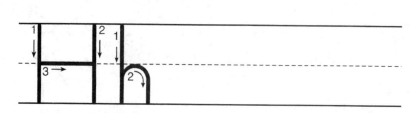

hens

hats

Hens have hats.

FS-32062 Beginning Manuscript Handwriting

Ii

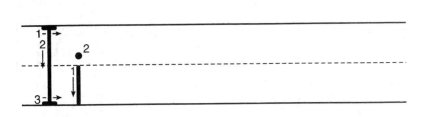

My Best

Ivan

Italy

Is Ivan in Italy?

1

Jj

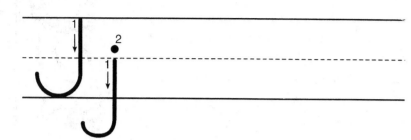

Jim

juggles

Jim juggles jars.

FS-32062 Beginning Manuscript Handwriting

Kk

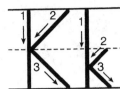

Katie

kick

Kangaroos kick.

Ll

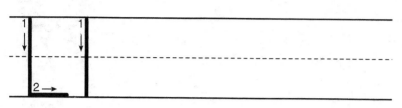

My Best

Lila

laughs

Lila laughs loudly.

Mm

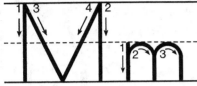

Meg

mud

Meg mixes mud.

FS-32062 Beginning Manuscript Handwriting

Nn

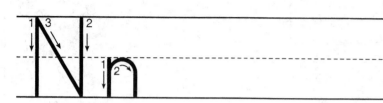

My Best

Nina

nuts

Nina nibbles nuts.

110

FS-32062 Beginning Manuscript Handwriting

Oo

My Best

Otto

oboes

Otto owns oboes.

Pp

P p

My Best

Paul

poppies

Paul picks poppies.

Qq

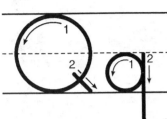

My Best
_____
- - - - - - - - - - -
_____

queens

quilt

Queens quilt quickly.

FS-32062 Beginning Manuscript Handwriting

Rr

rats

races

Rats run races.

Ss

My Best

Ss

Sue

soup

Sue sips soup.

Name_____

Tt

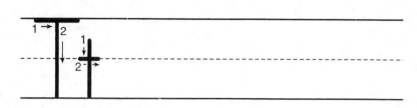

My Best

turtles

tiptoe

Two turtles tiptoe.

FS-32062 Beginning Manuscript Handwriting

Uu

| My Best |

U u

umpires

unite

Umpires unite.

FS-32062 Beginning Manuscript Handwriting

Vv

My Best

V v

Violet

Vern

Violet visits Vern.

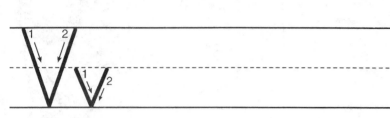

FS-32062 Beginning Manuscript Handwriting

Ww

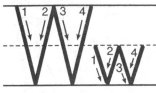

Wanda

worries

Wanda worries.

Name_____

Xx

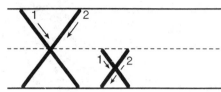

My Best

Xavier

x-rays

Xavier x-rays x's.

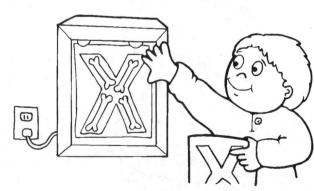

FS-32062 Beginning Manuscript Handwriting

Yy

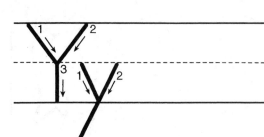

Yvette

yawns

Yvette yawns.

Name_____

Zz

My Best

Zach

zippers

Zach zips zippers.

© Frank Schaffer Publications, Inc.

FS-32062 Beginning Manuscript Handwriting

Days of the Week

Sunday

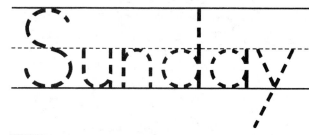

Monday   Tuesday

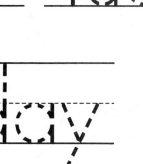

Wednesday

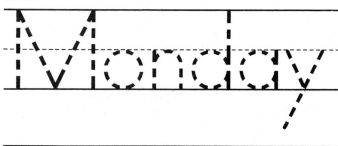

Thursday   Friday

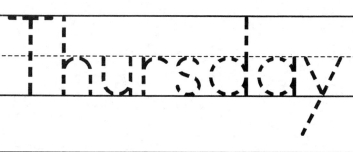   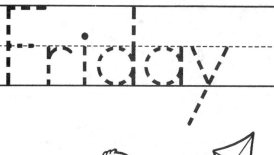

Saturday

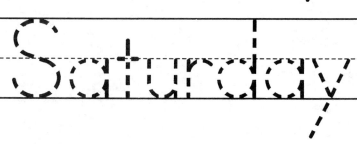   

Today is

_____

- -

Months of the Year

January

February

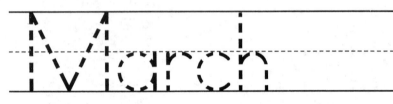

March

April

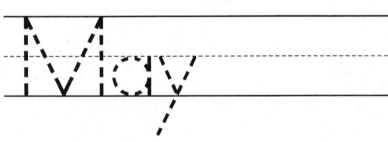

May

June

FS-32062 Beginning Manuscript Handwriting

Months of the Year

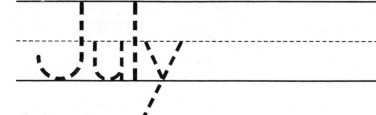

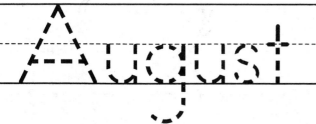

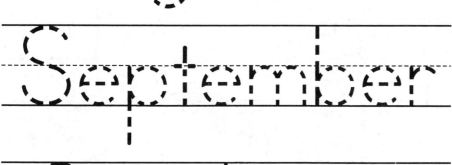

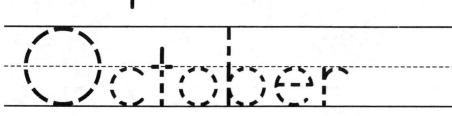

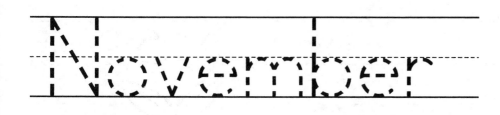

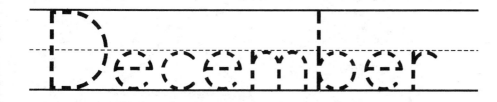

125

FS-32062 Beginning Manuscript Handwriting

Colors

red

blue

green

purple

yellow

orange

black

126

FS-32062 Beginning Manuscript Handwriting

What's My Name?

Write your first and last names in your very best handwriting.

Draw a picture of you practicing your handwriting.

FS-32062 Beginning Manuscript Handwriting

All the Letters

Copy this sentence neatly. It contains every letter of the alphabet.

The quick

brown fox jumps

over the lazy dog.